Reviving the Age-old Historical Tradition of India

By

Dr. Ravi Prakash Arya

Amazon Books, USA

In association with

Indian Foundation for Vedic Science

1051, Sector-1, Rohtak, Haryana, India, Pin-124001

Contact No. 9313033917; 9650183260

Email:vedicscience@rediffmail.com;

vedicscience@gmail.com

Second Edition

Kali era: 5119 (c. 2017)

Kalpa era : 1,97,29,49,119

Brahma era: 15,55,21,97,29,49,119

ISBN 9788187710394

Contents

Introduction

The westerners came here with the whole and sole mission to rule this country which was rich in all respects. They wanted to propagate their religion so that the people of this ancient most civilisation may also be converted into their fold. To rule this country politically, it was necessary for them to establish their racial, ideological and historical superiority upon the people of this country. That is why there was a deliberate attempt on the part of European intelligentsia in the 17th and 18th centuries to present a distorted picture of Indian history, culture and literature so that an intellectual crisis might be declared in this country. Under the cover of such a crisis they wanted to, as was done by Macaulay, enforce upon us their education so that Indians, bereft of their cultural richness and superiority in the past, might switch over to their faith and pave the way for their permanent settlement and rule in this country. As part of their plot against us, we were told that we don't have our own history except a few reminisces of the past in the name of history. It was told that we did not have any sense like that of history. Thus in a well-planned systematic way a crisis was declared by westerners regarding the absence of historical sense and history of this country. In fact, it was a plot against India and Indians. History is the soul of a country. If a country doesn't have her history, she becomes soul-less i.e. dead. A dead country can be ruled by anyone. Our history was distorted fact-wise and chronology-wise and confusion were created regarding the historicity of Indian history.

It's far more amazing to know that a person like William Jones, who was trying to conduct a fair study of Indian culture and history and could fix the entire chronology on the basis of the records of the Pur□ṇas, was persistently persuaded by the scholars like Max Müller, who had already concocted the theory of Aryan race with central Asia as their homeland, to demote the Indian chronology to such an extent as could prove the civilization of west far more ancient than that of India. This insistence of Max Müller (1859: p. 275) is reflected from his following observation:

> "There is but one means through which the History of India can be connected with Greece and its Chronology be reduced to proper limits. Although we look in vain in the literature of the Brahmaṇas or Buddhists for any allusion to Alexander's conquest, and although it is impossible to identify any of the historical events, related by Alexander's companions, with the historical traditions of India, one name has fortunately been preserved by classical writers who describe the events immediately following Alexander's conquest, to form a connecting link between the history of the East and the West. This is the name of Sandracottus or Sandrocyptus, the Sanskrit Chandragupta.

Max Müller's above-cited insistence forced William Jones to fall in line with him in misapplying the Greek synchronism of Sandracottus with Chandragupta of Maurya Dynasty instead of the Samudragupt of Gupta Dynasty.

The fact is that Itihāsa (history), in ancient times, was

studied as a science and was classified into 25 branches. It was given the status of the fifth Veda.

The present treatise sets aside all such accusations against India and Indian history as are unfounded and suggests some ways and means for the revival of the age-old historical tradition of Bhārata incorporated and preserved safely in Purāṇas, in the records of Pañjikāras existing at all the famous Tīrtha sthalas of India and in the traditions of Māgadhas and Sūtas, who were given the liability of teaching and preaching the history of our country. In this very chain Kathāvācakas, Cāraṇas, Bhāṭas, Mirāsis, Vṛttalekhakas' tradition may also not be overlooked who produced the literature based on real history.

Western Scholars' Plot

Having been acquainted with the vast and varied Sanskrit literature in 16th and 17th-century western scholars led by William Jones and others started giving their unfounded opinions out of prejudice on various aspects of Indian culture, civilization, and ancient most Vedic literature of the world. They came to India under the British imperialist forces with the whole and sole mission to rule this country which was rich in all aspects and to propagate their religion so that the people of this ancient most civilization may also be converted into their fold. In order to achieve this goal of theirs, Britishers hired needy and poor scholars like Max Mueller. Such scholars were given handsome remuneration to conduct the deep study of India and to present a distorted picture of the great Indian culture, history and civilization by twisting and manipulating the factual figures available in its copious and rich literature.

Max Müller, who served as a functionary for the colonialists, and for Christian evangelists, while being deeply interested in ancient Indian texts. This orientation is reflected in one of his letters addressed to the duke of Orgoil, who was the British secretary of state for India. Mueller wrote on 16 December 1868:

> 'The ancient religion of India is totally doomed and if Christianity doesn't step in whose fault will it be.'

In a letter addressed to his wife Georgina Adelaide Müller on December 9, 1867, Prof. Max Müller wrote

(Georgina Adelaide Müller, 1902: p. 328):

> 'I still have a great work to do, and I often feel that I might have done a great deal more if I had kept the one object of my life more steadily in view. I sometimes wish you would help me more in doing that, and insist on my working harder at the 'Veda' and nothing else. I hope I shall finish that work and feel convinced that though I shall not live to see it, yet this edition of mine and translation of Vedas will hereafter tell to a great extent on the fate of India and on the growth of millions of the souls in this country.'

He further observes (ibid.)

> 'It is the root of their religion, and to show them what the root is, I feel sure, is the only way of uprooting all that has sprung from it during the last 3,000 years '

The text of his letter is self-explanatory to the fact that Max Mueller started studying Sanskrit with ulterior motives and he was more or less successful in his efforts. Not only Max Mueller but also other European scholars were also hard-pressed by the Church on one hand and Darwin's pseudo-scientific theory of evolution on the other hand. Monier Williams (1879: Modern India and Indians, p. 262) writes:

> 'Christianity has many more points to their ancient faith than Islam has, and when the walls of the mighty fortress of Brahmanism are encircled, undermined and finally stormed by the soldiers of the cross, the victory of Christianity must be signal and complete.'

In his preface to his famous Sanskrit-English Dictionary (P ix, 1899) Monier William, as the Professor of Boden Chair, reveals the objective of founding the Chair for Sanskrit studies by Col. Boden as to convert the natives of India to Christianity. He writes thus:

> In explanation I must draw attention to the fact that I am only the second occupant of the Boden Chair, and that its founder; Col. Boden, stated most explicitly in his will (dated Aug. 15, 1811) that the special object of his munificent bequest was to promote the translation of the scriptures into Sanskrit; so as to enable his countrymen to proceed in the conversion of the natives of India to the Christian Religion.

Here I wouldn't like to blame the whole community of the then European scholars until and unless some concrete evidence has come across regarding their bias against Indian literature and their work to evangelise India. This is also a well-established fact that the European scholars who were not leading the mission like that of Max Mueller were persuaded by the pseudo-evolutionism of Darwin and by the conjectured propositions of their evangelical bosses like Archbishop Usher who declared that Earth originated 4004 years before Christ on Feb. 22 at 9 A.M. Since the Vedas were first ever written composition of the world, they were looked upon as the songs of the primitive shepherd or uncultured and savage race of the world and their age couldn't be fixed prior to 2000 BC or so. Thus from the aforementioned discussion, it can be informed that European scholarship was suffering from three serious defects.

Firstly it was their evil designs.

Secondly, they were not able to come out of the pressure of the Church. We know about many scholars like Galileo who had to pay for his life for seeking or accepting the truth. Everybody knows about the dictum prevalent in the fundamentalist Europe that so far as the Bible is concerned, Sun revolves around the Earth and so far as the Science is concerned, Earth revolves around the Sun.

The third thing coming to their way was their lack of understanding of the vast and exalted Sanskrit literature and as well as their total unfamiliarity with the tradition and culture of India.

All these three factors led to the distortion of Indian culture and literature at the hands of European scholars knowingly or unknowingly. These scholars also declared openly that history is non-existent in India. To quote a few, a German scholar M. Winternitz (1927: P. 30) in his Introduction to his reputed work 'A History of Indian literature' observes as follows:

> 'To them, the facts themselves were more important than their chronological order. They attached no importance at all, especially in the literary matters, to the question of what was earlier or later.'

An Arabian traveler, Alberuni (Edward C. Sachau, P.10), who in the year 1030 wrote a book on India remarks:

> 'Unfortunately, the Hindus do not pay much attention to the historical order of things. They are very careless in relating the chronological

> succession of their kings and when they are pressed for information, they are at loss, not knowing what to say, and invariably take to romancing.'

A. Macdonell (1900: P.7) also draws our attention to the same weakness of Indian literature.

> 'History is one weak spot in Indian literature. It is, in fact, non-existent. The total lack of historical sense is so characteristics, that the whole course of Sanskrit Literature is darkened by the shadow of this object, suffering as it does from an entire absence of exact chronology'.

According to Max Müller (1859: P. 18)

> 'No wonder that a nation like India cared so little for history?'

Major Willford (Ghasi Ram, P. 19) also leaves no stone unturned. He declared:

> 'With regard to history, the Hindus have really nothing but romances from which some truth occasionally may be extracted.'

Thus in a well-planned systematic way a crisis was declared by westerners regarding the absence of historical sense and history of India and Indians. In fact, it was a plot against India and Indians. History is the soul of a country. If a country doesn't have its history, it becomes soul-less i.e. dead. A dead country can be ruled by anyone. The main aim of foreigners was to rule this country. So, it was mandatory on their part to teach us that we don't have our history. With this slogan, they played an inexcusable game with us. They distorted our history fact-wise and chronology-wise. It will appear highly amazing to know that on one hand, some westerners were proclaiming that Indians had no sense of presenting the events chronologically. To them, the facts themselves were more important than their chronological order. On the other hand, William Jones, who started conducting a fair study of the Indian literature, could fix the entire chronology on the basis of the records of the Purāṇas. We get the following information from the Jones' treatise of 13 volumes (captioned as the Works of William Jones) in the chapter on The Chronology of the Hindus.

> 'And for these generations (Brahaddradhas) the Hindus allot a period of one thousand years. They reckon exactly the same number (1000 years) of years for twenty generations of Jarāsandha, whose son Sahadeva was contemporary to Yudhisthira, and founded a new dynasty in Magadha or Bihar. Then there is a list of twenty Magadha kings from Sahadeva, son of Jarāsandha to Satyajit, whose son Purañjaya is killed by his minister Sunga who placed his son Pradyota on the throne. Then the Pradyota dynasty starts in 2100 B.C., and then, the Śiśunaga Dynasty from 1962 B.C. followed by Nanda Dynasty from 1602 B.C. Then comes the Maurayas from 1502 B.C., the Sung dynasty, from Puṣyamitra 1365 B.C., to Kṣema Bhūmi 1253 B.C., then the Kanwa Dynasty from 1253 B.C. to 908 B.C., followed by the Andhra Dynasty from 908 B.C., to 452 B.C., the last king being Chandrabīja".

The above information from William Jones' treatise repudiates Westerners' accusations that Indians had no sense of writing history, or chronologically narrating the events. We had a clear-cut chronology assigned to each and every event of history. But it was a well-planned attack by the westerners to eradicate India's past. That is why to mislead Indians, they didn't approve of the authenticity of Paurāṇika and other historical records. Had they approved of the authenticity of Paurāṇika and other historical records preserved in Sanskrit literature, they would not have been able to declare the absence of history in India and the historical sense of Indians. It is far more amazing to know that William Jones was persistently persuaded by Max Mueller to demote the Indian chronology to such an extent as could prove the civilization of the west far more ancient than that of India. This scheme of Max Mueller of demoting Indian chronology deliberately is exposed by his following urge made to William Jones as under:

> "There is but one means through which the History of India can be connected with Greece and its Chronology be reduced to proper limits".

Max Müller's insistence forced William Jones to line up with him in misapplying the Greek synchronism of Sandracottus with Chandragupta of Maurya Dynasty instead of the Gupta Dynasty. Actually, Gupta Chandragupta flourished in 327 B.C. and was contemporary of Alexander. Maurya Chandragupta lived in 1534 B.C., but the western historians wrongly identified Alexander's contemporary with Maurya Chandragupta, thus reducing the chronology of Indian history by 1200 years. Furthermore, this declaration deleted another 1000 years because the modern history of Bharat Varsha starts with the Mahābhārata war in 3138 B.C., 36 years before Kali Era which started in 3102 B.C.

This colossal blunder terribly upset the whole chronology of Indian history bringing it to a near collapse. When this correction is made, every detail provided in the Purāṇas and other historical records will correspond with coupled with astronomical data will be found absolutely correct and one obtains a true picture of the history of India.

The western scholars wanted Indians to think of their history as per their wishes and to place the events of Indian history as per their preconceived chronological order. In other words, they wanted the dating of events or literature or litterateurs and kings in the framework of the well-planned plot against India and Indians hatched by them.

In fact, in their culture, the concept of chronology evolved only after the Jesus Christ 2000 years ago taught them the lessons on morality and civilization having learnt the same from the then Buddhists of India. Since then they accepted the Birth date of Christ as the sheet anchor in the historical chronology of the world. In fact, they wanted to preach in the light of the false Biblical view that Christ was the son of God born first on earth. St. Augustine through Hegel was impressed by Christian fundamentalism and sectarian bias. Karl Jaspers (1963: p.1), the writer of "The origin and goal of history" reveals this fact as:

> 'In the western world, the philosophy of history was founded in the Christian faith. In a grandiose sequence of works ranging from St. Augustine to Hegel, this faith visualized the movement of God through history. God's acts of revelation represent the decisive dividing lines.'

The Hegel could still say:

> "All history goes toward and comes from Christ. The appearance of the son of God is the axis of world history. Our chronology bears daily witness to this Christian structure of history."

Thus they started calculating the genesis or origin of all events and things after or before the birth of the first son of God, the Christ and vainly claimed themselves as the father of history. Historian philosophers like Jaspers (1963: p. 11) criticises the idea of history writing based on the Christian faith. According to him,

> 'But the Christian faith is the only one faith, not the faith of mankind. This view of universal history, therefore, suffers from the defect that it can only be valid for believing Christians. But even in the west, Christians have not tied their empirical conceptions of history to their faith. An article of faith is not an article of empirical insight into the real cause of history, as being different in its meaning.'

In fact, our western friends had no idea that the concept of chronology or Kālagaṇanā finds its origin with the very origin of the universe. They kept finding in ancient Indian literature the traces of Christian chronological dating type system and so couldn't understand the astronomical dating of the events. Astronomical dating, to them, appeared, as it does, in real sense romances and nothing else. They couldn't make out Kalhaṇa's dating of the Mahābhārata war. i.e. Saptarshi Saṁvat 628. i.e. 3138 B.C. To them, Vāyupurāṇa's dating of Nanda's accession in the Saptarshi Saṁvat 1015 (according to Patna school) i.e.

453 B.C. and in Saṁ. 610 (according to Kashmiri school) i.e. 453 B.C. had no meaning. Varamihira's unfolding his own time period i.e., 2625 years after the Yudhiṣṭhira's rule, i.e. 3138-2625=513 BC went unnoticed by them. Rama's birth in 24th Tretā Yuga at the junction of Treta and Dvāpara i.e. 181 lakh years ago doesn't satisfy their evangelical guidelines. Rāmāyaṇa's date appears to the modern scholars to be quite speculative and unbelievable. However, the recent excavations in archaeology have proved this date more or less to be true. Since we find the mention of four-tusked elephants in the Ramayana. The archaeological excavations have proved the existence of four tusked elephants about 15 million years ago. The below-given details are sufficient to prove the above fact.

Sources of Indian History

So far as sources of the history of Ancient India are concerned, we have a vast Sanskrit literature as source material to accomplish this uphill task. Today we have more than 15-lakh Sanskrit Manuscripts spread over the whole world. The need is to edit and publish such a huge number of books and to undertake an in-depth study of this work. Maharishi Dayanand Sarasvati in his celebrated work Satyaarth Prakash rendered a genealogy of the Kings ruled over in Indraprastha since the time of great emperor Yudhiṣṭhira. He borrowed this list from fortnightly papers Harischandra Patrikā and Mohan Patrikā that produced this genealogy based upon some 300 years old manuscript.

Kalhaṇa also while writing the chronology of the kings of Kaliyuga in his Rājataraṅgiṇī points out that the history of the Kaliyuga kings was crisis-ridden and he composed this work after collecting the data from many other sources that existed prior to him in fragmentary or in-tact forms. Thus there is no dearth of source material to compile the integrated history of ancient India if proper, genuine and painstaking efforts are made by scholars, institutions and the Indian Govt.

So far as the western historians or their spiritual children in India are concerned, these most accurate and proper Indian sources have no importance and validity. They appear to them like their mentors as romances. That is why, they didn't try to include in the history of ancient India the chapters on Harischandra, Raghu,

Yayati, Sharyati, Mandhata, Prithu, Shivi and hundreds of such others. Even the Ramayana and Mahābhārta periods do not form part of ancient Indian history. Our students have not been given to study history about Rama and Krishna whose birth dates are intact preserved till date and celebrated in Indian society with gaiety and fervor. But the paradox is that what was to be taught in the name of history is being studied in the name of myths, tales, or stories. For the westerners, no fact is reliable until and unless it is encoded in their accounts and their followers in India are destined to accept only what is stated by their foreign mentors. If Magasthenese writes a few words about India, the Mauryan empire becomes one of the chapters of Indian history and Sandrokotus quoted by him is falsely is recognized as the Greek synchronism for Indian Chandragupta Maurya. If Fah-I-Yan writes something about India, the Gupta period becomes another chapter of Indian history. If Heun-Tsang had something to say about India, Harshvardhana becomes the subject of study in Indian history. If an Arabian writer reminisces his stay in India or Babar writes his memoirs of India, they are accepted as historical documents. If Mortimer Wheeler or John Marshall excavate a mound in Harappa that becomes the foremost chapter of Indian history. Though Indus valley civilization was counted to be as old as c. 2600-1900 B.C. but the 5000 years old period of Mahābhārata has nothing to do with history. We are not ready to accept what is well established by our own sources. For us, Indian seers or scholarship has become unreliable and foreign scholarship provides valid pieces of evidence. In fact, we shall have come out of the clutches of foreigners if we want to write the actual integrated history of India.

We should take the foreign or archaeological sources as supportive pieces of evidence and not as the basic sources to formulate our history. If something is not available we shouldn't take it for granted that the wanted information is lacking. The actual problem is that a huge number of Indian sources were destroyed by foreigners and extant sources are also not with us in their intact forms. Maximum of the source material is also lying unnoticed by us in the museums and libraries of the world. The need is to explore and exploit this huge data bank for the formulation of the actual and factual history of India.

The Indian concept of History

Indian tradition studies history as a science and not as an art. Our ancestors called history Itihāsa Śāstra. History was a science because it dealt with the creation or the origin of the universe and the history of creation is related to science. That is why the Itihāsa and Purāṇas were called as fifth Veda.

इतिहास पुराणं पंचमो वेदः

Itihāsa purāṇam pañcamo vedaḥ.

Vedas are the name of the science of creation and the book dealing with the history of this science of creation will naturally be the scientific ones. Apart from the creation of the universe, history also dealt with the origin and expansion of mankind on this earth. As such history dealt with all the aspects related to the life of human beings and not only the political aspect as is the concept of modern history. In view of the same concept, several types of historiography developed in India. Indian historiography can be classified into 22 types.

1. Itihāsa

In ancient times in India history was studied, as told earlier, in altogether a different context from what it is today. The term used by ancient Indians was Itihāsa. The term history has evolved from Itihāsa itself. In fact, itihāsa was taken for a narration. The etymology of Itihāsa, i.e. iti ha vai āsa bears out the fact explicitly clear that Itihāsa is narrating a story. These days' narration is mostly used for the sake of amusement. We may hear old men narrating a story to children. But in ancient times, the narration didn't have the purpose of amusement; it had a more meaningful and more important purpose behind it. In the Vedic times, there emerged a school of Vedic interpretation which was known as the Aitihāsika school of Vedic interpretation. Aitihāsika school of Vedic interpretation, in fact, narrated figurative stories to elaborate and elucidate the creation of nature or of human beings. According to Durga, Itihāsa is that narrative that mainly traces the origin and cause of any important event.

निदानभूतमिति ह वै आसीदिति यत्रोच्यते स इतिहासः पुरावृत्त ख्यापकः समाचारः।

nidānabhūtaṁ iti ha vai āsiditi yatrocyate sa Itihāsaḥ purāvṛtta khyāpakaḥ samācāraḥ

(*Nir.* 2.10; 2.24; 9.23; 10.26, etc.)

Nirukta and Bṛhaddavatā employ the term Itihāsa or Ākhyāna while introducing some history in a figurative manner associated with the scientific fact revealed in Vedic hymns. Yāska in his Nirukta uses the term Itihāsa six times to denote such figurative legends as are narrated by Aitihāsikas. Earlier, Ākhyāna was the synonym of Itihāsa, but later on, it was distinguished from Itihāsa, since Itihāsa was taken in the broader sense which included various aspects of an Individual life in its purview, whereas Ākhyāna remained confined to the creation of universe only.

Thus Itihāsa has been used for the actual event that took place in the political or social sphere and thus Itihāsa became a fact rather than a fiction. This change in the meaning of Itihāsa later created confusion when the old dictum:

इतिहासपुराणाभ्यां वेदं समुपबृंहयेत् ।

Itihāsa purāṇābhyāṁ vedaṁ samupabṛṁyeta

That is, to explain and elucidate secrets of the Vedas by narrating the figurative legends (Itihāsa) and mysteries of creation or decreation unravelled in the Purāṇas) was studied in altogether a new context. Scholars had confusions regarding Vedas as having traces of actual political or social events.

In fact, Itihāsa was only the one aspect of the concept. The concept could find its completion when Purāṇa was also added to Itihāsa. So the duo of Itihāsa - Purāṇa was used everywhere. Now we shall discuss hereunder the meaning and scope of Purāṇa as viewed by ancient Indians.

2. Purāṇa

In fact, the term Purāṇa was used by ancient Indians in the sense of modern-day history or Itihāsa. The scope of Modern-day history is to record an event on political, social, or intellectual spheres in chronological order. Compare to modern-day history, the scope of Purāṇa was very vast and wide. Purāṇa was to deal with the five subjects.

सर्गश्च प्रतिसर्गश्च वंशो मन्वन्तराणि च
वंशानुचरितं चैव पुराण पंचलक्षणम् ॥

sargaśca pratisargaśca vaṁśo manvantarāṇī ca

Vaṁśānucaritaṁ caiva purāṇa pañcalakṣaṇam

1. Sarga: To maintain the connected account of the creation, or evolution of the Universe.

2. Pratisarga: To maintain the connected account of the decreation or dissolution of the Universe.

3. Varṁśa: To investigate the genesis and to maintain the record of descent of species.

4. Varṁśānucarit: To maintain the account of lineage or line of descent or pedigrees or genealogies till date.

5. Manvantara: To calculate and maintain the account of the time period since the time of the origin of the universe.

At the beginning of the origin of mankind, only the above-mentioned five issues were dominant and as such were subjected to the Purāṇa. Later, with the development and stratification of society, the issues concerning mankind were also stratified manifolds, and so the subject matter of Purāṇas also increased manifolds. The increased number of the subject matter of the Purāṇa is also cited in the various Purāṇas themselves. For instance, as per Śiva Purāṇa, the subject matter of Purāṇa should be as under:

सृष्टिश्चापि विसृष्टिचेत् स्थितिस्तेषां च पालनम् कर्मणा ।
वासना वार्ता चमूनां च क्रमेण च वर्णनम् ।
प्रलयानां च मोक्षस्य च निरुपणं च उत्कीर्तनम् ।
हरेरेव देवानां च पृथक् पृथक् ।

Sṛṣtiścāpi visṛṣtiścet sthitisteṣṁ ca pālanam karmaṇā

Vāsanā vārtā camūnāṁ ca krameṇa ca varṇanaṁ

Pralayānāṁ ca mokṣasya ca nirupaṇam utkīrtanaṁ

Hare reva devānāṁ ca pṛthak -pṛthak

The description of creation, decreation, sustenance, caring, action and attachment, an account of dissolution and redemption, and appreciation of psychological element and physical element also of various heavenly bodies are the subjects dealt with in the Purāṇas.'

Vāyu Purāṇa, on the other hand, gives a more elaborate account of the subject matter of the Purāṇas. It suggests:

> पुराणेषु बहवः धर्मास्ते विनिरुपिताः ।
> रागिणां च विरागाणां यतीनां ब्रह्मचारिणाम् गृहस्थानाम् ।
>
> वानप्रस्थानां स्त्रीशूद्राणां विशेषतः ॥
> ब्राह्मणक्षत्रियविशां ये च संकरजातयः ।
>
> गंगाद्या च महानद्या या महानद्यो यज्ञव्रत तपांसि च ॥
> अनेकविध दानानि यमाश्च नियमैः सह ।
>
> योगधर्माबहुविधाः सांख्याः भागवतस्तथा ॥
> भक्तिमार्गा ज्ञानमार्गा वैराग्यनिलनीरजः ।
>
> उपासनविधष्चोक्तं कर्म संशुद्धिचेतसाम् ॥
> ब्राह्मं शैवं वैष्णवं च सौरं शाक्तं तथाऽऽर्हतम् ।
> षड्दर्शनानि चोक्तानि स्वभावनियतानि च ॥
>
> एतदन्तच्च विधिं पुराणेषु निरूपितम् ।
> अतः परं किमप्यस्ति न वा बोद्धव्यमुत्तमम् ॥

Purāṇeṣu bahavo dharmāste vinirupitāḥ
rāgiṇāṁ ca virāgāṇāṁ yatīnā brahmacāriṇāṁ gṛhashānāṁ

vānprasthānāṁ striśūdrāṇāṁ viṛeṣataḥ
brāhmaṇa-kṣatriyaviśāṁ ye ca saṁkara jātayaḥ

gaṁgādayā ca mahānadyā yā mahānadyo yajña-vrata ṣ tapāṁsi ca

anekavidha-dānāni yamāśca niyamaiḥ saha

yogadharmā bahuvidhāḥ sāṁkhyā bhāgavatāstathā
bhaktimārgā jñānamārgā vairāgyanila-nīrajaḥ

upāsana vidhiścoktaṁ karma-saṁśuddhi cetasām
brāhmaṁ śaivaṁ vaiṣṇavaṁ ca sauraṁ śāktam tathā' rhatam

ṣaḍdarśanāni coktāni svabhāva niyatāni ca
etadantacca vividhaṁ putāṇeṣu nirūpitam

ataḥ paraṁ kimapyasti na vā boddhavyam uttamam
(Vāyu Purāṇa, 104.11-17.)

'Purāṇas are also the records of various ethical codes (dharmas) observed by lovers, recluses, ascetics, brahmacharis (bachelors taking to the study of Vedas and other Śāstras), householders, jungle-dwellers, ladies and particularly scholars, defence personnel, traders and fourth class people and other mixed professional races. Geographical accounts and accounts of various schools of rituals and religions and various other things concerning individual and society are the main subjects to be dealt with in the Purāṇas.'

Thus it is crystal clear from the foregoing discussion that Itihāsa, in ancient times, instead of recording the important events in chronological order, traced the origin and causes of important events that occurred in nature or society and maintained the connected account thereof in terms of time and space. In fact, Purāṇa dealt with all those events that repeat in every new creation. Hence it was said in connection with Purāṇas; *purā navaṁ bhavati iti Purāṇam*, 'Whatever repeats is the subject matter of Purāṇa'. Thus Purāṇa was the actual substitute of modern history. The etymology of Purāṇa is also very much akin to the dictum associated with history 'History repeats. Itihāsa and Purāṇa were the supplements of each other. Whereas Purāṇa recorded the events, Itihāsa traced the origin and causes of the recorded events.

3. **Ākhyāna:** was used, as stated above, for historical legend associated with the creation of the universe.

4. **Upākhyāna:** is a sub narration related to the main narration.

5. **Sarga**: Creation of the universe.

6. **Anvākhyana**: To relate the historical narration narrated by some other person.

7. **Ākhyāyikā**: A historical narration of creation traditionally handed down to posterity.

8. **Purākalpa:** To narrate the events took place in the previous kalpas.

9. **Purāvṛtta**: To narrate the events took place in the previous manvantaras.

10. **Aitihya:** A popular event in history.

11. **Itivṛtta**: A brief history.

12. **Parakriyā**: A style to narrate historically the historical works/ deeds done by others.

13. **Parakṛti:** A style to narrate the history recorded by another historian.

14. **Kathā**: The historical narration about the main character.

15. **Parikathā**: The historical narration of characters other than the main character.

16. Gāthā: There is difference between gāthā and kathā. Kathā is the historical narration about the main character, but gāthā is a narration told in the context of the main narration.

17. Charit: Biography of ideal leaders in the society.

18. Anucharit: Biography of the posterity of leaders in the society.

19. Vaṁśa: To investigate the genesis and to maintain the record of descent of species and heavenly bodies.

20. Vaṁśānucarit: To maintain the account of lineage or line of descent or pedigrees or genealogies till date.

21. Gotra-pravarakāra: An institution of individuals keeping an account of main gotras (descents) and subsequent gotras.

22. Nārāśaṁsī: To prepare a bibliography of the persons who have made a laudable contribution for the furtherance of the cause of the society or the nation.

23. Rājaśāsana: Recording of political history.

24. Kālavida: An astronomer keeping the record of the history of time and chronology in history.

Now the question arises as to what steps may be taken today for the preservation and furtherance of the age-old scientific tradition of Itihāsa and Purāṇa of India?

(1) To revive the age-old tradition of Itihāsa, we shall have to trace the origin and causes of events we are dealing with. We are to describe actions in terms of tendencies, motives, causes and ends behind them.

(2) To revive the tradition of Purāṇa, we shall have to collect, consolidate and compile the data on the

evolution and dissolution of the universe lying scattered in the Vedic texts and present the connected account of the same in the more lucid and simple terms or say in modern scientific terms, we shall have to trace the descent of heavenly bodies. We shall have to restructure our calendar as per calculation done by Vedic Ṛṣis which is more scientific and begins with the very beginning of our universe. We shall have to trace the connected account of origin and evolution of speech.

(3) We shall have to preserve the records of Pañjikāras existing at all the famous Tīrtha sthalas of India. Through the records of Pañjikāras we are still able to know at least 1000 years long history of each and every village of this country and the people inhabiting there.

(4) We should also take steps to preserve the traditions of Māgadhas and Sūtas who were given the liability of teaching and preaching the history of our country. In this very chain Kathāvācakas, Cāraṇas, Bhāṭas, Mirāsis, Vṛttalekhakas' tradition may not be overlooked who produced the literature based on real history.

Historical Eras of the World

Indian eras as on 2017

Brahma Era (Vedic Era for Universal creation): 155, 521, 972, 949,119 (155 trillion year)

Kalpa or Sṛṣṭi Era (Vedic Era for biological Creation on Earth): 1,972, 949,119 (1.97 billion years)

Human creation on Earth: 1, 960,853,119 (1.96 billion years)

Manvantara Era: 120, 533,119

Tikha Saṁvat: 6925

Saptarṣi Saṁvat: Ardra 93 or 5193 (starts from Māgha Śukla 9)

Yudhiṣṭhir Saṁvat: 5191

Kaliyuga Era: 5119 (starting from Dakṣīṇāyana i.e. 21st June)

Buddha Saṁvat: 3854 (starting on May 23)

Old Mahavir Nirvāṇa Saṁvat: 2544 (Starts on Kārtika Amavaśyā)

Vikramī Saṁvat: 2074 (Starting on Caitra Śukla 1)

Śākā Saṁvat: 1940 (starting on Phalguna Śukla 12)

Kalchuri Saṁvat: 1766

Vallabhi or Gupta Saṁvat: 1700

Harsha Saṁvat: 1411

Nanakshahi Saṁvat: 549 (starting on March 15)

Khalsa Saṁvat: 319 (starting on April 13)

Dayanand Saṁvat: 135 (Starting on Kārtika Amavaśyā)

Other eras of the world as on 2017

Old Chinese Era : 96, 002,513 (96 million years)

Hittite Era : 88, 840, 389 (88.8 million years)

Chaldean Era : 2, 150, 049 (2.1 million years)

Persian Era : 189,983

Finishian Era : 30,019

Egyptian Era : 28,680

Turkish Era : 7,623 years

Irani Era : 6,020 years

Jewish Era : 5,777 years

New Chinese Era : 4,373 years

New Turkish Era : 4,307 years

Greek Era : 3,587 years

Roman Era : 2,766 years

Christian Era : 2017 years (January 1)

Hizri Era : 1,439 years (Muhurram 1)

Epoch of Rāmāyaṇa

Yogavāsiṣṭha supplies the information regarding the time period of Rāma. In this connection the following śloka may be referred to

अद्य राम कृते क्षीणे त्रेता सम्प्रति वर्तते - *6/1.27.18*

adya rāma kṛte kṣīṇe tretā samprati vartate.

[Meaning] Now, O Rama, now Satyayuga has gone by and we are in tretā yuga when you are born to subdue your enemies.

From the above statement, it is clear that during Rāma's time Satyayuga had elapsed and Tretā was in currency. According to the information from Mahābhārata, Rāma was was born in the sandhi period of Dvāpara and Tretāyuga. Presently 28th Kaliyuga is in currency. As such the 28th Tretāyuga has passed.

However Puranic sources give more specific information. Accordingly, Rāma was born in the 24th Tretāyuga. This period works out, given astronomical calculations, to be around 18 Million years. The calculations are as under:

Years of 28th Kaliyuga elapsed	=5120
Years of 28th Dvāpara elapsed	=864,000
Years of 28th Tretā elapsed	=1,296,000
Years of 28th Satyayuga elapsed	=1,728,000
Years of 27th Mahāyuga elapsed	=4,320,000
Years of 26th Mahāyuga elapsed	=4,320,000

Years of 25th Mahāyuga clapscd	=4,320,000
Years of 24th Kaliyuga elapsed	=432,000
Years of 24th Dvāpara elapsed	=864,000

Total years at the end of Tretā	= 18149120
Years of 24th Tretā	= 129600
Total years at the beginning of Tretā	= 17072661

Accordingly the birth of Rāma took place from 17.072,661 (1.7 million) years to 18,149,120 (1.8 million) years ago from 2019 AD (Kali 5120).

We have some more specific astronomical information about the birth of Rāma from Rāmāyaṇa (1.18.8-9) which is rendered below:

ततो यज्ञे समाप्ते तु ऋतूनां षट् समत्ययुः ।
ततश्च द्वादशे मासे चैत्रे नावमिके तिथौ ॥ 8॥
नक्षत्रे अदितिदैवत्ये स्वोच्चसंस्थेषु पंचसु ।
ग्रहेषु कर्कटे लग्ने वाक्पताविन्दुना सह ॥ 9॥
प्रोद्यमाने जगन्नाथं सर्वलोकनमस्कृतम् ।
कौसल्याजनयद् रामं दिव्यलक्षणयुतम् ॥ 10॥

And when the six seasons had rolled away after the completion of Yajña, in the 12th month of Chaitra on the 9th lunation; in the'Punarvasu' constellation presided over by the Aditi devatā; when the five planets were in their uccha (mandoccha), i.e. the Sun, the Jupiter, the Saturn, the Mars, and the Venus were in their Mandoccha (Apsis). Mandoccha of Bṛhaspati had arisen with Moon at Karka (Cancer) ascendant (Lagna), Kausalya gave birth to Rama.

This information has confused some scholars. Here it may be mentioned that Mrs. Saroj Bala a retired IRS officer is spreading confusion over last many years regarding the date of birth of Śri Rāma. According to her (Dating the Era of Lord Ram, Rupa & co. Delhi, 2005), Śri Rāma was born on 10th January 5114 BC. She claims that she is getting these results on the basis of Planetarium Gold software and also produces a sky view of planetory positions as given by the software. Planetarium and the other softwares are not able to predict the mandoccha (apsis) of the planets and tell you about the Indian lunar months existing during that period. Here it may be informed that planetory positions of planets as suggested by the above author based upon the misunderstanding of the śloka of Rāmāyaṇa. Even if we go by this misunderstood concept, these positionsare not taking place on 10th January 5114 BC. Even a laymen knows that the Sun never enters Aries sign in January. In 5114 BC the Sun used to enter Makara sign on 27th Jan., so on 10th Jan. 5114 BC, the sun was in Dhanuu sign. When sun is in Makara or Dhanu sign, there may be either Pauṣa or Māgha months. So, there is no question of commencement of Chaitra month in January. On careful examination of the Horoscope of 5114 BC, prepared with the help of Astrodienst, one will find that on 10th January 5114 BC position of various stars according to tropical (See Horoscope 1) and sideareal (See Horoscope 2) calculations is as under:

Name of Star	Position (Tropical)	Position (Sidereal)
Sun	Sagittarius	Aquraius
Jupiter	Gemini	Leo
Mars	Aquarius	Aries

Name of Star	Position (Tropical)	Position (Sidereal)
Venus	Sagitarus	Pisces
Saturn	Leo	Scorpio

Horoscope 1

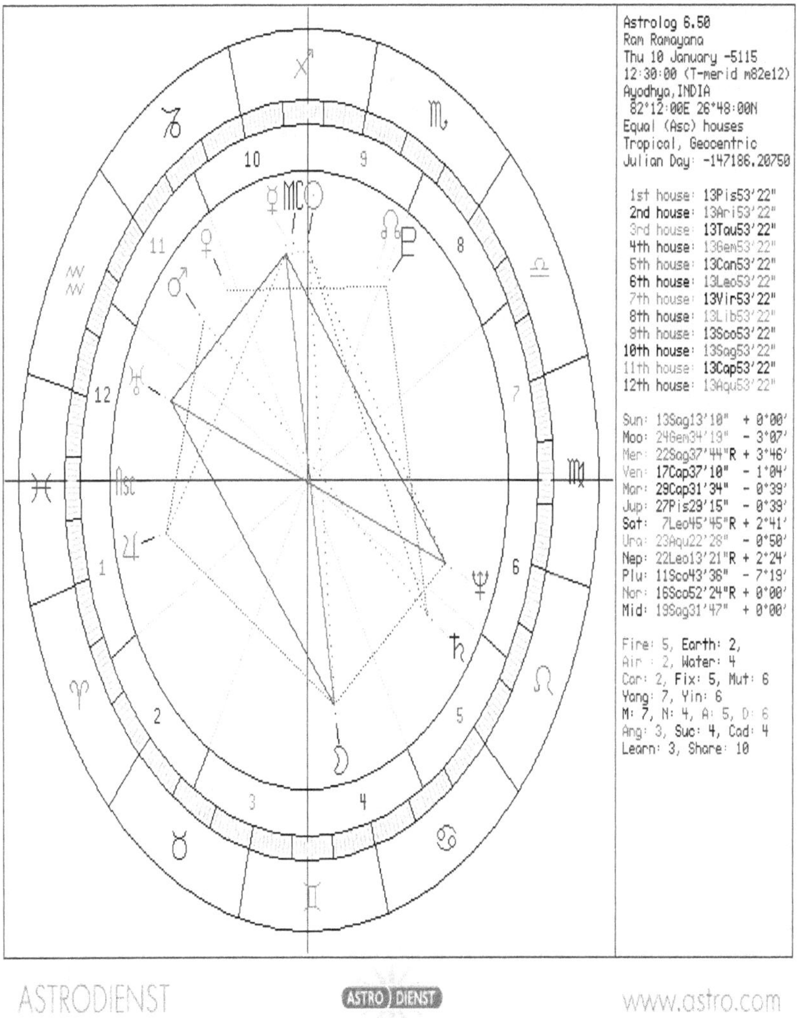

Horoscope 2

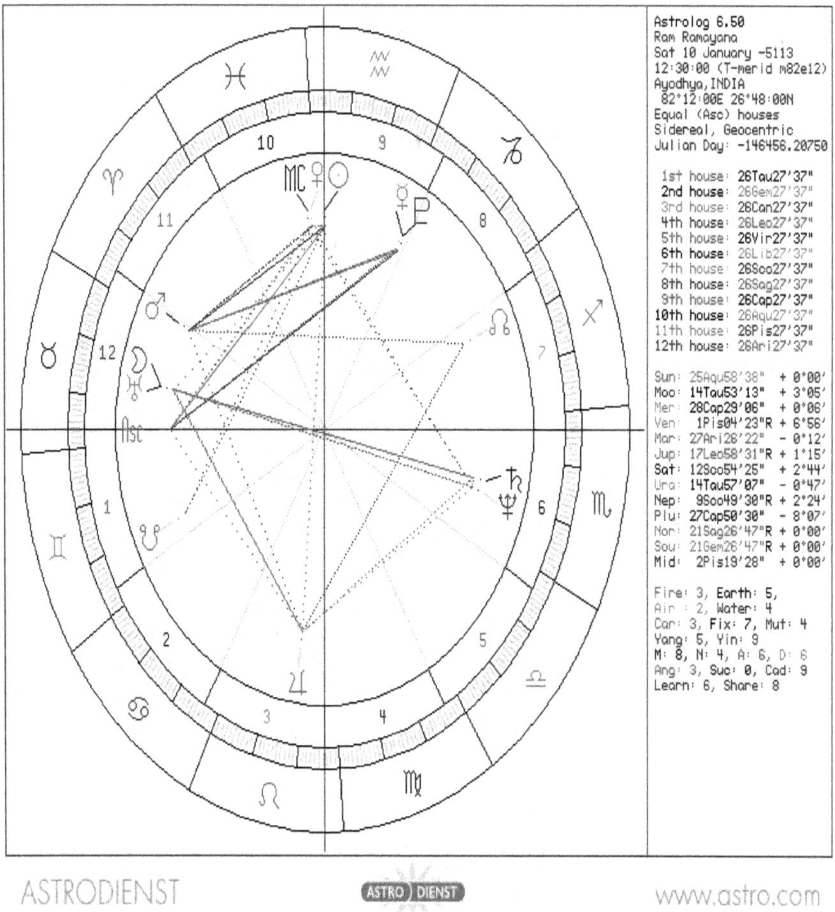

So none of planetory positions as wrongly taken to mean from the śloka of Rāmāyaṇa actually tallies with the postions claimed by Saroj Bala. Moreover, as pointed out above her translation of Ramayaṇa's śloka is also a farfetched one based upon the misunderstanding of the meaning. In the śloka the mention of the word 'uccha' word in connection with grahashas been wrongly translated as the 'uccha' position of grahas as is considered in astrology. Here the author of Rāmāyaṇa is not talking about astrology, but astronomyto fix the date line of of Rāma. So, here 'uccha'stands for the mandoccha (highest slow speed) of the grahas. The author of Rāmāyaṇa gives two hints, 1. By the time of the birth of Rāma, the lagna (ascendent) Karka (Cancer) was on the rise, and 2. The Moon and Mandoccha of Bṛhaspati was also rising in Karka sign, which was also the ascendent of during that period. 3. The Moon was in conjuction with Punarvasu Nakṣatra of Karka sign. Here it may be clarified that 4th quarter of Punarvasu Nakṣatra spends in Karka Sign. The Longitude of Kakra sign is from 900 to 1200 and the longitudes of Punarvasu Nakṣatra are 800-93.20. So the 4th quarter of Punarvasu spending time in Karka sign has longitudes from 900-93.20. So, according to the above mentioned information mandoccha of Bṛhaspati has to be between 900-93.20 Here it may also be known that when a planet or graha is at its mandoccha (apsis) at 00 or 3600 and 1800, defference of its true and mean position is also 0. According to Bhāskarāchārya, mandoccha of Bṛhaspati completes 855 revolutions in a period of Kalpa (4,320,000,000 years) and according to present Sūrya Siddhanta mandoccha of Bṛhaspati takes 900 revolutionsin a Kalpa year (i.e. 4,320,000,000 years minus 17064000 years of creation[1]=) 4302936000 years.

---

1 According to present Sūryasiddhānta, all planets came at 0 degree in Aśvinī Nakṣatra along with their apsis and nodes after lapse of 17064000 years of the commencement of the present

But Bhāskarāchārya or Brāhma Siddhānta does't assume any period any period spent over creation, like the present Sūrya Siddhānta. Hereunder, we shall perform calculations according to both the Siddāntas.

According to Bhāskarācharya, one revolution of Bṛhaspati's mandoccha will take place in 4,320,000,000/855= 5052631.5789473years. As per Paurāṇika sources, already quoted above, Rāma's birth took place in 24th Tretāyuga. We know that till the beginning of 24th Tretāyuga 1,936,440,000 years had passed since the beginning of the Kalpa. So, dividing the 1,936,440,000 years by 5052631.5789473 years, we get the position of Bṛhaspati's mandoccha in the beginning of 24th Tretāyuga as (1,936,440,000 / 5052631.5789473=) 383.25375. It would mean that Bṛhaspati's mandoccha has completed 383 revolutions by the beginning of 24th Tretāyuga and had moved .25375X360=91.35 degrees, which is the position of Punarvasu Nakṣatra in Karka Sign. This is a solid proof of

---

Kalpa. Otherwise their conjunction with Aśvinī Nakṣatra started from the very beginning of the Kalpa. They conjunct with Aśvinī Nakṣatra every 1080000 years. When they completed 15 cycles of their conjunction in 4 Mahāyugas and were meeting again for the 16th times after the lapse of 17064000 years of Kalpa, in the middle of the Kaliyuga, the conjuction of their apsis and nodes also took place with them. So, this period of 17064000 years is taken as the period of creation in Sūryasiddhānta. Brāhma and other Siddhāntas are silent about it. So, when revolution of planets or their conjunction in Aśvinī Nakṣatra is considered, the period of Kalpa should taken as 4,320,000,000. But when the revolutions of their apsis (mandoccha) and nodes (śighroccha) is considered the period of Kalpa should be counted as 4,320,000,000 -17064000= 4302936000 years.

the exact dateline of Śri Rāma as per Yogavasiṣṭha that Śri Rāma was born in the beginning of 24th Tretayuga, i.e.17.072,661 (1.7 million) years ago from 2019 AD). It appears that Yogavāsiṣṭha's calculation is according to Brāhma Siddhānta adopted by Bhāskarāchārya. But if we do this calculation according to the present Sūryasiddhānta the time of Rama's birth comes at the end of 24th Tretā yuga. The calculations are as under:

According to Sūrya Siddhānta, as quoted above, one revolution of Bṛhaspati's mandoccha will take place in 4,302,936,000/900= 4781040 years. We know that till the beginning of 24th Tretāyuga 1,936,440,000 years had passed. So, dividing the 1,936,440,000 years by 4781040 years, we get the position of Bṛhaspati's mandoccha in 24th Tretāyuga as (1,936,440,000 / 4781040=) 405.0248481502. It would mean that Bṛhaspati's mandoccha has completed 405 revolutions by the beginning of 24th Tretāyuga and had moved .0248481502X360=8.94 degrees, which is the position of Aśvini Nakṣatra in Meṣa Sign. Punarvasu Nakṣatra in Karka sign is at 900. The difference between two is 90-8.94 = 81.054665928 degrees. Bṛhaspati's mandoccha takes 4781040/360=13280.9999677 years to travel one degree. So, Bṛhaspati's mandoccha will take 81.054665928 x 13280.9999677 = 1,076,459 years to reach the 4th pāda of Punarvasu Nakṣatra in Karka sign. Calculations according to present Sūryasiddhānta show that Rāma was born at the end of Tretā yuga, i.e. 17,072,661+1,076,459= 18,149,120 (1.8. million) years ago from 2019 AD). It appears that

In addition to the above astronomical evidence, we have some other literary and archaeological evidence to support this view. It is also mentioned in Purāṇas that by Rāma's time, the last phase of the Himalayan upliftment was also over. The above fact is corroborated by the internal evidence of Rāmāyaṇa and archaeoloigcal findings. In Vālmīki Ramāyaṇa (Dr. Ravi Prakash Arya, 1998)[2], Sundara Kāṇḍa (4.28), it is mentioned that when Hanumāna first reached Rāvana's palace, he saw decked gateways surrounded by four-tusked elephants resembling the masses of white clouds and wild beasts and birds. The verse goes like this:

वारणैश्च चतुर्दन्तैः श्वेताभ्रनिचयोपमैः।

भूषितैः रुचिरद्वारं मत्तैश्च मृगपक्षिभिः॥

vāraṇaiśca chaturdantaiḥ śvetābhranicayopamaiḥ

bhūṣitaiḥ ruciradvāraṁ mattaiśca mṛgapakṣibhiḥ.

[Meaning] The inner apartments of Rāvaṇa were adorned with four-tusked elephants resembling masses of white clouds; and possessing graceful gateways attended by deer and chirping birds.

At another place (Rāmāyaṇa, Sundara kāṇḍa, 27.12), Trijaṫā, a Rākṣasī, sees in her dream illustrious Rāma and Lakṣamaṇa mounted on a huge elephant with four tusks resembling a hill. The original verse reads as un*der*:

राघवश्च पुनर्दृष्टश्चतुर्दन्त महागजम्।

आरूढः शैलसंकाशं चकास सहलक्ष्मणः॥

rāghavaśca punardṛṣṫaśchaturdanta mahāgajam
ārūḍhaśailasaṅkāśaṁ chakāsa sahalakṣamaṇaḥ

---

2 Dr. Ravi Prakash Arya (1998). Vālmiki Rāmayaṇa edited with English Translation, (Four Vols.), Delhi

[Meaning] I saw again Lakṣamaṇa appear in effulgence, seated on a huge elephant, having four tusks and resembling a hill.

Mention of four-tusked elephants by Vālmīki is glaring evidence of the fact that elephants with four tusks must have been present during the period of Rāmāyaṇa and Vālmīki. The Encarta Encyclopaedia informs us about the presence of four-tusked elephants on earth between 38 million years ago to 15 million years ago. They are named as Mastodontoidea. Accordingly, Mastodontoidea evolved around 38 million years ago and became extinct about 15million years ago when the shaggy and two tusked Mastodons increased in population.

The above proof lends strong support to the authenticity of the tradition of Purānas. Now one may easily understand that the astronomical time calculation system adopted by Vedic seers is only the key to the true chronology of India history. Modern historians calculations are quite misleading and are proof of their misunderstanding of the Indian knowledge system.

Four tusked elephant of Rāmāyaña

The paradox with such historians was that they don't have the adequate knowledge of astronomy or Kālagaṇanā. The fact is that the study of ancient Indian history would not be complete until and unless one is well-versed in astronomy and Sanskrit. Even today, it would be advisable to the students of ancient history to have an additional qualification in astronomy or Kālagaṇanā and Sanskrit. Historians unqualified in Kālagaṇanā and Sanskrit would not be able to do the justice with the ancient Indian history; rather they would make a mockery of it.

Non-existent of history is not the weakness of Indian literature, but the actual weakness of the reviewers. There is a dictum in Sanskrit.

नैष स्थाणोरपराधो यदेनमन्धो न पश्यति

Naiṣa sthaṇoraparādho yadainam andho na paśyati.

'It is not the weakness of the pillar if a blind man cannot see it. The actual weakness lies within the blind person.'

The Indian concept of history was much more scientific than we have it today. Indians not only try to record the births, deaths and posterity of kings, but there was the provision to register the birth, death and posterity of even a layman in the society. This tendency is still prevalent which is centred around the famous Tīrtha sthalas of the country. Go to Hardwar, Allahabad, Srinagar and other holy places, you will find their Paṇḍas or Pañjikāras or Registrars who are maintaining the history of laymen by recording their birth, death and posterity at their own level without any help and support from Govt. It is surprising to know that Maithala Brāhmaṇas in Bihar have a tradition of getting the records of seven generations verified by the institution of Pañjikārās before the betrothal ceremony. This all points out to the deep sense of history prevalent among the common men in Indian society.

The Epoch of Śri Kṛṣṇa

51/7/28th Dvāpara/863875/Bhādrapada/K-8

Or 24 Sept. 3226 BC (Julian Calendar)

In the Bhāgavatam (11.6.25), Brahmā informs that Krishna remained on the earth for 125 years.

यदुवंशेऽवतीर्णस्य भवतः पुरुषोत्तमः ।

शरच्छतं व्यतीयाय पंचविंशाधिकं प्रभो ॥

Puruṣottama Krishna born in Yadu Dynasty lived for 125 years.

We are well informed that Śri Krishna died by the end of Dvāpara yuga or the beginning of Kaliyuga. He was born on 8th lunation of the dark half of Bhādrapada month in Rohini Makshtra. If we add 125 years to 3101 BC., the date of commencement of Kaliyuga. Śri Kṛṣṇa's birth date will be 24Sept. 3226BC, Friday or 51/7/28th Dvāpara/863875/Bhādrapada/K-8. The calculations are as under:

3rdSept. 3226BC, Thursday	Śrāvaṇa Amāvasyā
18th Sept. 3226 BC, Friday	Sun ingresses in Kanyāsign
17thSept. 3226 BC, Thursday	Bhādrapada Pūrṇimā
24thSept. 3226BC, Friday	Bhādrapada K-8
2ndOct. 3226 BC, Friday	Bhādrapada Amāvasyā

On 24th Sept. 3226 BC (-3225 Julian), at the time of Krishna's Birth at 12 O clock midnight Moon was 23^0 14' in Vṛṣabha Rāśī which means that Moon was in 4th Pāda of Rohini Nakshtra, as 4th pāda of Rohiṇī Nakṣatra is located from 20^{0}- 23^{0}.20'in Vṛṣabha Rāśī.

The Epoch of Yudhiṣṭhira's Coronation

51/7/28th Dvāpara/863928

or 3173BC (Julian Calendar)

Kaliyuga acts as the milestone in determining the chronology of Indian history prior and post Mahābhārata war. After fixing the date of commencement of Kaliyuga, it becomes easy to fix the dates of various other events of Indian history. There are many astronomical and literary evidence to help us. The 14th verse of Kaliyuga Rāja Vṛttānta asserts:

पंचसप्ततिवर्षाणि प्राक्कलेः सप्त ते द्विजाः ।

मघास्वासन् महाराजे शासत्युर्वीं युधिष्ठिरे ॥

The Sapta Rishis (the Great Bear) entered the asterism of Maghās, just 75 years before the beginning of Kaliyuga,i.e. 3176 BC.The great king Yudhiṣṭhira ruled the earth during the said period in 3173 BC.

The Bṛhat Saṁhitā (13.3) quoted by Kalhaṇa (1148 AD) in his work called 'Rājataraṅginī', (1.56) informs that Yudhiṣṭhira ruled the country when Saptarṣis were posited in Maghā Nakṣatra. The verse reads as under:

आसन् मघासु मुनयः शासति पृथिवीं युधिष्ठिरे नृपतौ ।

षड्द्विक्पंचद्वियुतः शककालस्य राज्यस्य ॥

When the King Yudhiṣṭhira ruled the earth, Munis (the Great Bear) stood in Maghā constellation. Now by the time of Varāhamihira, 2526 years of Yudhiṣṭhira Śaka (starting from 3173BC) have elapsed. It gives the time period of Varahāmihira 3173-2526= 647 BC.

Kaliyuga Rāja Vṛttānta (Bhaviṣya Purāṇa, Chapt. 3) also informs that after the lapse of 25 years in the Kaliyuga (3101 BC), the Saptarṣīin their retrograde motion will enter Āśleṣā star (in retrogade motion) and stay there for hundred years.

पंचविंशतिवर्षेषु गतेष्वथ कलौ युगे।

समाश्रयिष्यन्त्याश्लेषां मुनयस्ते शतं समाः ॥

Our calendar proves this fact.

The king Yudhiṣṭhira's coronation took place 36 years before the Mahābhārata war in 3173 BC when Saptarishis completed 3 yearsin Maghā Nakṣatra.Saptarishis entered Maghā Nakṣatra 75 years before Kaliyuga on 1st lunation of bright half of Chaitra month 3176 BC. The fact that Saptarishis entered Maghā Nakṣatra in 3176 BC can be verified from the following evidence on record.

Saptarishis entered Maghā nakṣatra on Chaitra S-1. Calculations prove that this happened on 27th March, 3176 BC Saturday. Calculations are as under:

1.	26 March 3176 BC, Friday	Phālguna Amāvasyā
2.	27th March 3176 BC, Saturday	Chaitra S-1
3.	16th April 3176 BC, Friday	Sun ingresses in Meṣa sign
4.	9th April 3176 BC, Tuesday	Chaitra Pūrṇimā
5.	25th April 3176 BC, Sunday	Chaitra Amāvasyā

One of the leading Indologists Prof. Weber on the

basis of the tradition of Kashmiri Pandits and other evidence concluded that Laukika Saṁvat came into vogue on the 1st lunation of the bright half of Chaitra month when 25 years of Kaliyuga were elapsed. In 3076 BC Kaliyuga completed 25 years and Saptarishis entered P. Phalguni Nakṣatra. According to this calculation Saptarishis spent 75 years in Maghā Nakṣatra in Dvāpara yuga and 25 years in Kaliyuga. Babu Shyam Sunder Das writes in 'Prāchina Lekhāvali' that Śāstra Saṁvat started in 824 AD. Here Śāstra Saṁvat indicates the Saptarṣi Saṁvat. Our'7000 Years Calendar of Various Indian Eras' clearly shows that in 824 AD. new Saptarṣi Saṁvat started with the entry of Saptarṣis in DhaniṣṭhāNakṣatra.

Kalhaṇa (1148 AD) in his Rājatariṅgiṇī (1.52) observes that at present in 24th Laukika Saṁvat,Śaka (Śālivāhana) Saṁvat1070 is in currency. While going through our table, one finds that Saptarishis are posited in Uttarabhādrapada 24. The original verse reads as under:

लौकिकेऽब्दे चतुर्विंशे शककालस्य साम्प्रतम्।

सप्तत्यभ्यधिकं यातं सहस्रं परिवत्सराः॥

At present in the 24th Laukika Era, 1070 years of Śaka Saṁvat have elapsed.

This gives Kalhaṇa's epoch to be 1148 AD.

1. In 1486 Vikrama Saṁvat, a stotra of Bhavani Jwalamukhi was engraved on a stone by Raghava Chaitanya during the reign of Raja Sansāra Chand son of Karma Chand and grandson of Raja Prem Chand of Trigarta Kangra. This stone registers 5th year of Laukika Saṁvat. On examination of our table, one finds that in 1486 Chaitrādi Vikrama Saṁvat, Saptarishis were spending their 5thyear in Bharaṇīasterism.

2. Two inscriptions have been excavated in Baijanath, which were written in Chaitrādi Vikramaera 861 during the period of Raja Jaichand of Kangra and Raja Lakṣmaṇachand of Kairgaon of Himachal Pradesh by Rāma son of Bharnatraka. One of the inscriptions, mentions 80th year of Laukika Saṁvat and another mentions Śaka Saṁvat 726. The authenticity of these dates can be easily verified from our table which gives us to understand that Chaitrādi Vikramaera 861 corresponded with Śaka (Śalivāhana) Saṁvat 726 and at that time Saptarṣis were spending an 80th year in Śravaṇa Nakṣatra.

3. Babu Shyam Sunder Das mentions in 'Prāchina Lekhāwali' that Laukika Saṁvat commenced on completion of 1681 Chaitrādi Vikramaera. Our 7000 Years Calendar gives one to understand that after the completion of 1681 Chaitrādi Vikrama era, Saptarṣis completed their sojourn in Kṛttikas and entered in Rohiṇi Nakṣatra which proves that a new laukika Saṁvat commenced after completion of 1681 Chaitrādi Vikrama era.

4. The Raja Abhaya Chand and some other Rajputs installed a Jain Murti in the market place of Kangra, Himachal Pradesh in Chaitrādi Vikramaera 1811. A rock inscription was also installed there wherein laukika Saṁvat 30 is mentioned. Our table gives one to understand that in Chaitrādi Vikramaera 1811, Saptarishis were enjoying their 30th-year sojourn in Mṛgaśirā Nakṣatra.

5. Raja Śri Singh Deva of Chamba had a copper plate written. It registers Laukika Saṁvat 34. It can be verified from our table that in Chaitrādi Vikrama era 1915,

Saptarishis were spending their 34th year in Ārdrā Nakṣatra.

6. One more inscription of the same king is available dating Chaitrādi Vikramaera 1916, which registers Śāstra Saṁvat 35, i.e. Ārdrā 35.

The above shreds of evidence are sufficed to prove that Saptarishis entered Maghā Nakṣatra 75 years before Kaliyuga, i.e. 3176 BC.

Here it may not be out of context to inform that Saptarishi Saṁvat may not have its astronomical significance, but it had its significance for chronology. Varahamihira does speak of it. If the astronomer Varāhamihira makes mention of Saptarishis' movement for 100 years in each nakṣatra, it is with reference to chronology. It was called 'Śāstra Saṁvat' because it dealt with the chronology of the Śāstras and ancient Indian history. It was also called 'Laukika Saṁvat', because it was easy for the common man to maintain a record of 100 years and restart the counting after completion of 100 years.

The Epoch of Mahābhārata War

51/7/28th Dvāpara/863963/Kārtika Pūrṇimā

or 20th Nov. 3137 BC (Julian Calendar)

Aihole inscription [3] of Meguti Templerecords the dates of two events, Mahābhārata war and defeat of king Harsha by Chalukya ruler at the hands of Rāṣtrakūṭa king Dantidurga in 78 AD. The inscription reads as under -

त्रिंशत्सु (30) त्रिसहस्त्रेषु (3000) भारताद् आह्वादितः ।
सप्ताब्दशतयुक्तेषु (107) गतेष्वब्देषु पंचसु (5) ॥
पंचाशत्सु (50) कलौ काले षट्सु (6) पंचशतासु (500) च ।
समासु समतीतासु शकानाम् भूभुजाम् ॥

[Meaning] 30 + 3000 + 107= 3137 years from Bhārat war have passed. Means the current year is 1 AD. From the years that have passed in Kali yuga, 5+50+6+500=561 years of Śaka rulehavealso passed. It points out to some Saṁvat that started in 561 BC. It means that Ravikīrti constructed the temple

---

[3] Many inscriptions are found at Aihole, one of the most important is the inscription at Meguti Temple, popularly known as Aihole inscription, or Aihole Prashasti (Eulogy) of the Chalukya king Pulakeshi-II. The inscription uses Sanskrit language and is written in Kannada script. There is a mention about the defeat of King Harshavardhana (Vikramādtya II (82 BC-19 AD) by Pulikeshi II in the inscription. There is also a mention about the victory of Chalukyas over the Pallavas and the shifting the capital from Aiholeto Badami by Pulakeshi-II. The poet Kalidasa (of Jyotirvidābharaṇa) finds mention in the inscription and this matches with their timings.

in 1 AD.

The year 3137 BC matches with the period mentionedin Mahābhārata. The history in Mahābhārata goes like this. After the coronation at Indraprastha, Yudhiṣṭhira set out to perform the RājasuyaYajña. Arjuna, Bhīma, Nakula, and Sahadeva led armies across the four corners of the world to subdue the kings all over the world and fetch tributes to the emperor. The non-compliant Magadha king, Jarāsandhawas defeated by Bhima and Krishna. At his Yajña, Yudhiṣṭhira chose Krishna as his honoured guest. Thus he successfully completed 23 years of his rule till 3150 BC. However, Yudhiṣṭhira fell a prey to Shakuni's tactics and entangled with him in the game of dice. He lost his kingdom, his brothers and wife. While playing for the second time, he lost all his kingdom in the game and was forced into exile for 13 years, which included one year in anonymity till 3137 BC. When the period of exile was completed, Duryodhana refused to return his kingdom. Yudhiṣṭhira made numerous diplomatic efforts to retrieve his kingdom peacefully but in vain. At last, he was forced to wage a war against the tyrant Duryodhana.

We are informed from Mahābhārata that Krishna saw the signs of the destruction of Yadvas as Gāndhārī burning with grief on account of her sons and deprived of all her kinsmen by the end of the Mahābhārata war cursed him that his kinsmen Yadavas will also be perished fighting themselves after 36 years. The verses go like this:

एवं पश्यन्हृषीकेशः संप्राप्तं कालपर्ययम् ।

त्र्योदश्याममावास्यां तान्दृष्ट्वा प्राब्रवीदिदम् ॥

चतुदर्शी पंचदर्शी कृतेयं राहुणा पुनः ।

तदा च भारते युद्धे प्राप्ता चाद्या क्षयाय नः ॥

विमृशन्नेव कालं तं परिचिन्त्य जनार्दनः ।

मेने प्राप्तं स षट्त्रिंशं वर्षं वै केशिसूदनः ॥

पुत्रशोकाभिसंतप्ता गान्धारी हतबान्धवा ।

यदनुव्याजहारार्ता तदिदं समुपागतम् ॥ महाभारत, 16.3.16-19

Behold these signs that indicated the inauspicious course of timeand seeing that the day of new moon coincided with 13th lunation, Hṛṣikeśa summoning the Yadvas, said unto them these words- The fourteenth lunation has been made the 13th by Rāhū once more. Such day had appeared at the time of the great battle of the Bharatas. It has once more appeared, seem, for our destruction. The slayer of Keśī, thinking upon the omens that time showed, understood that the 36th year had come and that what Gāndhārī, burning with grief on account of the death of her sons and deprived of all her kinsmen, had said was about to transpire.

Similarly, at another place in Mahābhārata, the popular king Yudhiṣṭhira is depicted to take into account of the inauspicious omens after the lapse of 36 years of Mahābhārata war. The description goes like this:

षट्त्रिंशे त्वथ संप्राप्ते वर्षे कौरवनन्दनः ।

ददर्शविपरितानि निमित्तानि युधिष्ठिरः ॥

आदित्यो रजसा राजन् समवच्छन्नमण्डलः ।

विरश्मिरुदये नित्यं कबन्धैः समदृश्यत ॥ महाभारत, 16.1.1; 4

When the 36th year began, the popular Kuru king, Yudhiṣṭhira, saw inauspicious omens. The sun's disk looked covered with dust all over and destitute of splendour.

There is also a reference in the Mausala Parva of Mahābhārata (2.19-20) that there also occurred a solar eclipse in the 36th year after Mahabharata war (20th Nov. 3137 BC-9th Feb. 3137 BC) following which Dwarka submerged under the sea. We find that a Partial Solar Eclipse occurred on 31stAugust3101 BC exactly in the 36th year of Mahābhārata war which may also be considered the period of submergence of Dwarka under sea.

The above-cited references of the Mahābhārata give clinching evidence of the date of the great war of Bharat as around 36 years before the commencement of Kaliyuga (28th Sept. 3101 BC). After 36 years of the great war of Bharat close to the end of Dvāpara or the beginning of Kaliyuga, Yudhiṣṭhira left the throne of Hastinapur for Parikṣita to rule. Yadvas also perished in the family or dynastic feud and Śri Krishna also left for heavenly abode. Keeping in view of all these facts and some more references from Mahābhārata are worth quoting.

1. There is a reference in the Mahābhārata (Bhiṣma Parva, 3.29) that there was a lunar eclipse followed by a solar eclipse in the same month, before the actual war. It may here be informed that this astronomical phenomenon took place in July 3137 BC. On the Āṣāḍha Pūrṇimā, the 25th July 3137 BC, there occurred a Total Lunar Eclipse followed by a Partial Solar Eclipse in the same month i.e. Āṣāḍha Amāvasyā on 9thAugust, 3137 BC.

2. Śri Kirshna proceeded to Hastinapur on a peace

mission to avoid war on Kārtika Śukla Pratipadā.

ततो व्यपेते तमसि सूर्ये विमल उद्गते ।

मैत्रे मुहूर्ते संप्राप्ते मृद्वर्चिषि दिवाकरे ॥

कौमुदे मासि रेवत्यां शरदन्ते हिमागमे ।

स्फीतसस्यसुखे काले कल्पः सत्त्वतां वरः ॥ महाभारत, 5.81.6-7

Then, when Śarada season had ended and Hemanta season was just beginning (14Nov. 3137 BC), in the month of Kumuda (Kārtika) on the constellation of Revati, when the darkness of night was over, and the clear sun appeared, on Maitra Muhurta that well disposed (or ever ready hero of the heroes set off in the tender rays of the sun for Hastinapur.

The time described above is the month of Kārtika when the darkness of the night was over. It means that the time was Kārtika S-1. As per our calculations the positions of Amāvasyā, Pūrṇimā and the sun's ingress were as under:

6th Nov. 3137 BC, Saturday	Āśvina Amāvasyā
7th Nov. 3137 BC, Sunday	Kārtika S-1
15th Nov. 3137 BC, Saturday	The sun ingressed into Vṛśchika sign
20th Nov. 3137 BC, Saturday	Kārtika Pūṛṇimā
6th Dec. 3137 BC, Monday	KārtikaAmāvasyā

Thus Kartika S-1 occurred on 7th Nov., 3137BC, Sunday.

But when the peace mission failed due to the adamant stance of Duryodhana, the war was declared on Kārtika Purṇimā, i.e. 20th Nov. 3137 CE, Saturday, which is 13 days after the peace mission. I quote the exact reference from Mahābhārata (6.2.23-24). The reading is given as under:

> अलक्ष्यः प्रभया हीनः पौर्णमासीं च कार्त्तिकीम् ।
>
> चन्द्रोभूदग्निवर्णश्च समवर्णे नभस्तले ॥
>
> स्वप्स्यन्ति निहता वीरा भूमिमावृत्य पार्थिवाः ॥
>
> Vyāsa describes the ill-omens. O! Dhṛtarāṣṭra on the full moon of the night of Kārtika, the moon was hardly visible, devoid of glory, with firish tinge, (and) both the horizons were of the same hue. The ground was completely covered by the bodies of the kings killed in the war, lying there.

Here it may be informed that the war took place in two phases. The sequence is as under:

Kārtika Pūrṇimā or 20th Nov.3137 B.C. Saturday: The first phase of the war started on 20th Nov. 3137 BC. It lasted for 10 days, i.e till Kārtika K-9 or 29th Nov.3137 BC. Wednesday.

Kārtika K-9, or 29th Nov. 3137 B.C. Mārgaśīrṣa S-6or 10th Dec. 3137 BC Friday: There was a cease-fire for 12 days.

Mārgaśīrṣa S-6, or 10th Dec. 3137 B.C. Mārgaśīrṣa S-14 or 19th Dec. 3137 BC Sunday: The second phase started on 10th Dec.and ended after 8 days on Mārgaśīrṣa S-14 or 19thDec.3137 BC., Sunday. We have a complete sequence of other events in Mahābhārata. Some of the important events are cited below:

Māgha S-8, or 9 Feb., 3136 B.C. Monday: Bhiṣma Pitāmaha died after 56 days battling on Śara Śayyā.

Hereunder, we provide a proof from the Mahābhārata demonstrating that Bhiṣma left for heavenly abode on the 56th day after his fall in the battlefield on 8th day of bright half of Māgha month.

Epoch of Commencement of Kaliyuga

51/7/28th Kaliyuga/1/Bhādrapada/ K-13

or 28th Sept. 3101 BC (Julian), Friday

The Saṁkalpa Pāṫhas prevalent all over India describe the time period and the place where a particular event is taking place. Saṁkalpa Pāṫhas collected from all over India shows uniformity in time. Accordingly, 2019 AD corresponds to 5120th year of Kaliyuga which shows that Kaliyuga started 5119 years before in 3101 BC. French mathematicians and astronomers like J. Sylvain Bailly (1736-1793) and Mr. Le Verrier (1811-1877), the discoverer of the planet Neptune concluded that the present Kaliyuga commenced at the midnight of ending 17th and beginning of 18th Feb. in 3102. But the Indian astronomical tradition says that present Kaliyuga commenced on midnight of Bhādrapada K-13, Friday during the period of Āśleṣā constellation. Astronomical calculations are as under: (Note: below given dates are as per Julian Calendar)

31st August 3101 BC, Friday	Śrāvaṇa Amāvasyā
17th Sept. 3101 BC, Monday	Sun ingressed in Kanyā sign
14th Sept 3101 BC, Friday	Bhādrapada Pūrṇamāsī
30th Sept. 3101 BC, Sunday	Bhādrapada Amāvasyā
28th Sept. 3101 BC, Friday	Bhādrapada K-13

Thus, we can say with the perfection that Kaliyuga started on midnight of ending 28th and beginning 29th September 3101 BC. on Friday. According to Āryabhaṭa (Āryabhaṭiyam, 1.5), Dvāpra Yuga ended with Thursday and the Kaliyuga began on Friday.

काहो मनवो ढमनुयुग श्ख गतास्ते च मनुयुगछ्ना च।

कल्पादेर्युगपादा ग च गुरुदिवसाच्च भारतात्पूर्वम्।

There are 14(ढ) Manus in a day of Brahman called a Kalpa, and 72 (श्ख) yugas constitute the period of a Manu. Since the beginning of this Kalpa by the end of Dvāpara yuga in which Mahābhārata war took place, 6 Manvantaras has elapsed, and of the current 7th Manvantara 27 (छ्ना) Yugas (Mahāyugas) have passed and of the current 28th Mahāyuga Satya, Tretā and Dvāpara yugas have also passed. The end of the Dvāpara yuga i.e.27th September, i.e. Bhādrapada Kṛṣṇa 12, 3101 BC was marked by Thursday.

According to the original Sūryasiddhānat of Pañchsiddhāntikā, Kaliyuga commenced at mid night on Thursay and Aryabhaṭa has assumed to it to begin at sunrise on Friday, that is 15 ghaṭis later.

References

1. Ali, S.M. (1966). Reprinted 1973. *Geography of Purāṇas.* People's Publishing House, New Delhi.
2. Edward C. Sachau (1910).*Alberuni's India*, 2nd edition, Kegan Paul, Tubner and Co., London
3. Edwin Bryant (2001). *The Quest for the Origins of Vedic Culture: The Indo-Aryan Migration Debate.* OxfordUniversity Press.
4. Georgina Adelaide Mueller (1902). The Life and Letters of the Right Honourable Friedrich Max Mueller, Longmans, Green, Vol.1
5. Ghasi Ram: *Maharṣi Dayanda ka Jeevan Charit*
6. Jaspers, Karl (1963).*The origin and goal of history,* New Haven and London, Yale University Press.
7. Kota Venktachalam (1956).*Indian Eras.*
8. Kota Venktachalam (1953).*Chronology of Nepal History.*
9. Kota Venktachalam(1953b).*The Plot in IndianChronology.*
10. Kota Venkatchalam (1955). The Chronology of Kashmir History Reconstructed.
11. Kota Venktachalam (1957). The *Chronology of Indian History,* Part 1 & 2.
12. Macdonell, A.A. (1900). History of Sanskrit Literature, D Appleton and Company, New York

13. Max Mueller (1859). *History of Ancient Sanskrit Literature, Williams and Norgate, London*Shri Ram Sharma (Edited): *Śiva Purāṇa*

14. Ravi Prakash Arya (2019): 7000 Years Old Calendar of Various Indian Eras. Indian Foundation for Vedic Science, Rohtak, Haryana.

15. Ravi Prakash Arya (2019 a): 7000 Years' Calendar of Lunar Months (7 vols), Amazon Books, USA

16. Shyam Manohar Mishra (1977). *Yaśovarman of Kanauj, A study of Political History, Social and cultural life of Northern India During the reign of Yaśovarman*, Abhinav Publications, New Delhi.

17. Śiva Purāṇa, edited by Shri Ram Sharma, Introduction, P. 11)

18. Skanda Purāṇa, Chaukhamba Prakashan, Sanskrit Series Office, Varanasi, 2019.

19. Vedveer Arya (2015). *The Chronology of Ancient India*, Aryabhata Publications, Hyderabad.

20. Williams, Monier (1879). English-Sanskrit Dictionary,

21. Williams, Monier (1879). '*Modern India and Indians,* Third Edition,Tubner and Co. London

22. William Jones (1799). *The Works of William Jones,* G.G. and J. Robinson, London

23. Winternitz, M(1927). '*A History of Indian literature',* Vol. 1', University of Calcutta.

www.ingramcontent.com/pod-product-compliance
Lightning Source LLC
Chambersburg PA
CBHW071733020426
42331CB00008B/2014
* 9 7 8 8 1 8 7 7 1 0 3 9 4 *